Table of Contents

Table of Contents

Table of Contents (cont.)

PREFACE

THIS BOOK PRESENTS A COLLECTION OF PICTURES AND DESCRIPTIONS OF THE AUTHOR'S FAVORITE INSECTS. IT CAN SERVE BOTH AS AN INTRODUCTION AND AS A WAY TO HELP IDENTIFYING THEM IN THEIR NATURAL ENVIRONMENT.

YOU MAY LEARN SOMETHING NEW ABOUT WELL-KNOWN INSECTS, AS THE BOOK BRINGS INTERESTING FACTS ABOUT THEM. YOU WILL ALSO LEARN ABOUT SOME NEWLY DISCOVERED ONES. FACT BOXES PROVIDE ADDITIONAL USEFUL INFORMATION ABOUT TAXONOMY, DISTRIBUTION AND SIZE.

THIS BOOK ALSO INCLUDES HAND-DRAWN ILLUSTRATIONS BY THE YOUNG AUTHOR, AN 11 YEAR-OLD BOY WHO IS VERY CURIOUS AND PASSIONATE ABOUT THEM. AT THE END OF THE BOOK YOU WILL FIND A LITTLE SURPRISE: SEE IF YOU CAN HOLD YOUR CURIOSITY AND WAIT UNTIL THE END...

HAVE FUN!!!

INTRODUCTION

Head
Thorax
Abdomen

INSECTS ARE A CLASS OF INVERTEBRATES WITHIN THE ARTHROPOD FAMILY THAT HAVE AN EXOSKELETON, A THREE-PART BODY (HEAD, THORAX AND ABDOMEN), THREE PAIRS OF JOINTED LEGS, COMPOUNDED EYES AND ONE PAIR OF ANTENNAE.

THEY ARE AMONG THE MOST DIVERSE GROUPS OF ANIMALS ON THE PLANET, INCLUDING MORE THAN A MILLION DESCRIBED SPECIES, REPRESENTING MORE THAN HALF OF ALL KNOWN LIVING ORGANISMS. THE NUMBER OF EXISTING SPECIES IS ESTIMATED AT BETWEEN SIX AND TEN MILLION, AND POTENTIALLY REPRESENT OVER 90% OF THE DIFFERENT ANIMAL LIFE FORMS ON EARTH.

INSECTS MAY BE FOUND IN NEARLY ALL ENVIRONMENTS, ALTHOUGH ONLY A SMALL NUMBER OF SPECIES RESIDE IN THE OCEANS, A HABITAT DOMINATED BY ANOTHER ARTHROPOD GROUP, THE CRUSTACEANS.

DEDICATED TO MY FAMILY AND FRIENDS

Bush Cricket

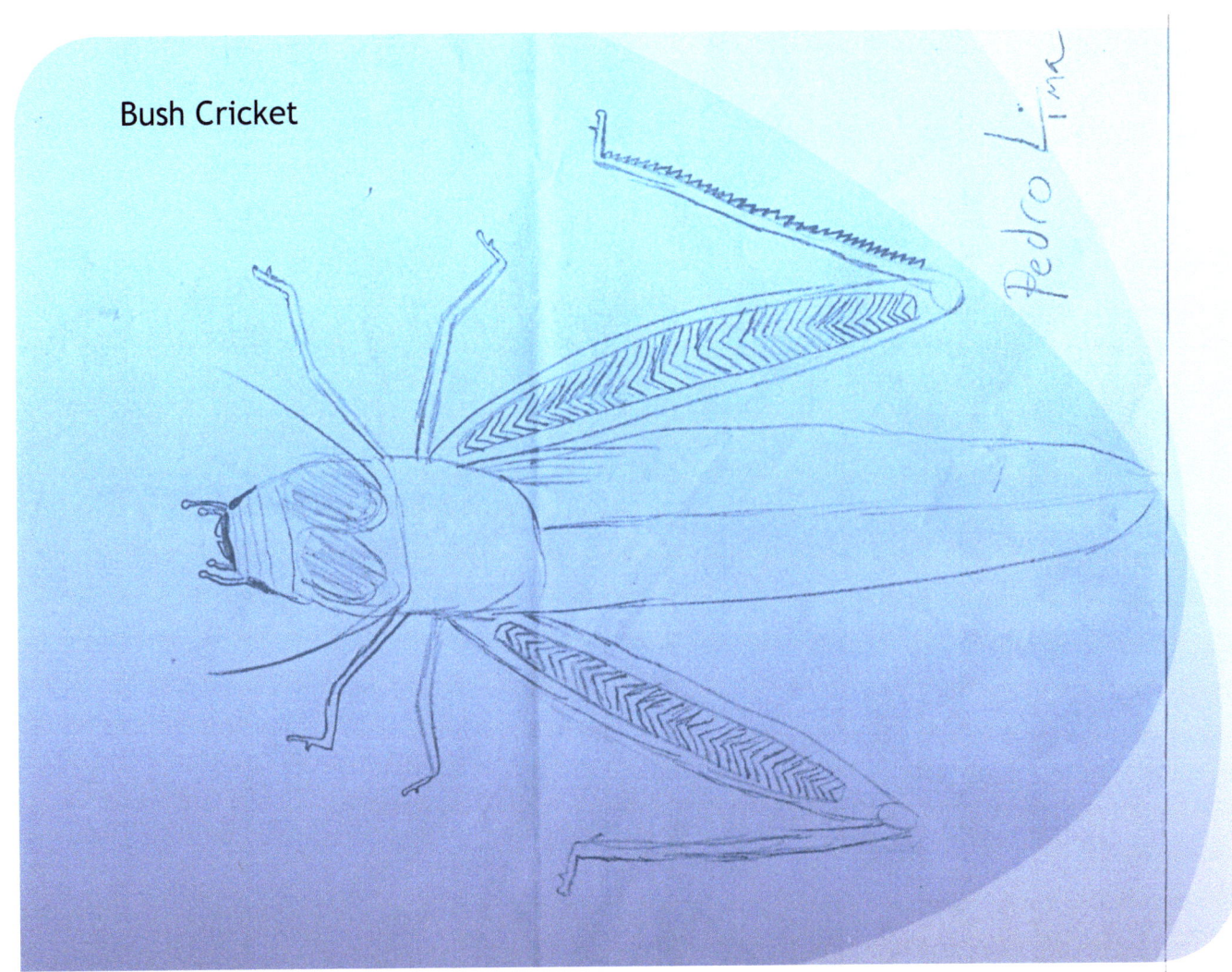

Pedro Lima

Azure Damselfly

Adult male Azure damselflies have a head and thorax patterned with blue and black. They have an azure blue abdomen patterned with black markings. The marking on the second segment of the abdomen is U-shaped, separated from the segment's narrow terminal black band. (This distinguishes it from the Variable Damselfly where the U-shape is joined to the terminal band with a black line.)

Blue Morpho

The Blue Morpho is an iridescent tropical butterfly found in Mexico, Central America, Trinidad, northern South America, and Paraguay.

The brilliant blue color in the butterfly's wings is caused by the diffraction of the light from millions of tiny scales on its wings. It uses this to scare away predators, by flashing its wings rapidly. The entire Blue Morpho butterfly lifecycle, from egg to adult, is only 115 days.

THE BLUEBOTTLE FLY

CALIPHORA VOMITORIA

The bluebottle fly or "bottlebee" (Calliphora Vomitoria) is a common blow-fly found in most areas of the world and is the type species for the genus Calliphora. Similar species include the greenbottle fly, a close relative that can be distinguished by its bright green metallic colouring. Bluebottle fly adults feed on nectar, while the larvae feed on carcasses of dead animals. Adults are also pollinators to some flowers with strong odor.

Centipedes

Centipedes, though not being insects but rather arachnids, are arthropods belonging to the class Chilopoda (subphylum Myriapoda). They are elongated metameric creatures with one pair of legs per segment of their body. Despite the name, centipedes can have a varying number of legs from under 20 to over 300. Centipedes have an odd number of pairs of legs, 15 or 17 pairs of legs (30 or 34 legs). Therefore, there is no centipede with exactly 100 legs. A key trait uniting this group is a pair of venom claws or "forcipules". Centipedes are predominantly carnivorous.

Cavernicolous and subterranean species may lack pigmentation and many tropical scolopendromorphs have bright aposematiccolours. Size can range from a few millimetres (in the smaller lithobiomorphs and geophilomorphs) to about 30 cm in the largest scolopendromorphs. Centipedes can be found hiding in a variety of environments such as under rocks, shoes and basements.

CENTIPEDES (continued)

Worldwide, there are estimated to be 8,000 species of centipedes, of which 3,000 have already been described. Centipedes have a wide geographical range, reaching beyond the Arctic Circle. Centipedes are found in an array of terrestrial habitats from tropical rainforests to deserts. Within these habitats, centipedes require a moist micro-habitat because they lack the waxy cuticle of insects and arachnids, and so lose water rapidly through the skin. They are also found in soil and leaf litter, under stones and dead wood, and inside logs. Centipedes are among the largest terrestrial invertebrate predators and often contribute significantly to the invertebrate predatory biomass in terrestrial ecosystems.

CICADAS

There are about 2500 species of cicadas in the world. They live on temperate and tropical regions. We almost never see cicadas larvae, because they live under ground. After mating, the female (typically) cuts a slit into the bark of a tree and lay eggs there. Then, nymphs fall on the ground and they will burrow into it.

DARK GREEN FRITILLARY

- The Dark Green Fritillary is the most widespread fritillary found throughout the British Islands, although it is less common in central and eastern England. It is a pleasure to see them as they fly powerfully over its grassland habitats, frequently stopping to nectar on Thistles and Knapweed. It gets its name from the green hue found on the underside of the hind wings, which are peppered with large silver spots.

- Outside of central Scotland and southern England, it is most frequently found in coastal areas and is the only fritillary found in Orkney and the Outer Hebrides. Despite its powerful flight, it is somewhat surprising that this butterfly is not particularly mobile, staying within its breeding grounds.

VIOLET DARTER/VIOLET DROPWING

o The violet dropwing (*Trithemis Annulata*) is a distinctive dragonfly that is well known for its striking violet coloration, from which it gets its common name. The male of this species appears purple, but this is due to a bright red base color on the abdomen and thorax, which is overlaid with a blue, powdery bloom on the surface, creating the vibrant violet coloration.

o The violet dropwing is a small to medium-sized dragonfly and has a distinctly broad abdomen. Like many other dropwing species, the violet dropwing immediately lowers its wings on landing, a behavior which gives this group of dragonflies their common name.

EMPEROR MOTH

THE SMALL EMPEROR MOTH (*SATURNIA PAVONIA*) IS A MOTH OF THE FAMILY SATURNIIDAE. SOMETIMES, THE INCORRECT GENUS NAME PAVONIA IS STILL USED FOR THIS SPECIES. THE EMPEROR MOTH LIVES IN TROPICAL REGIONS AND IN SOUTH ARCTIC CIRCLE SUCH AS NEARBY THE ENGLAND ISLANDS.

EMPUSID MANTIS

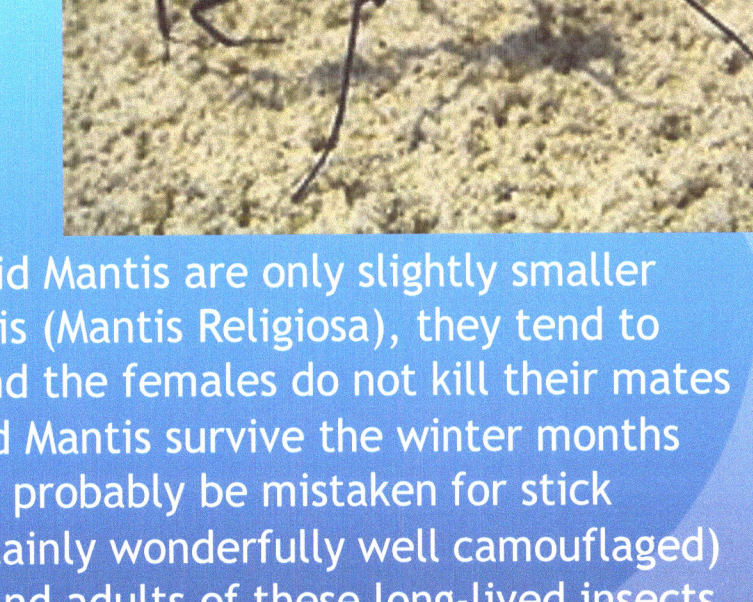

Although adult Empusid Mantis are only slightly smaller than the Praying Mantis (Mantis Religiosa), they tend to tackle smaller prey and the females do not kill their mates when pairing. Empusid Mantis survive the winter months as nymphs (these may probably be mistaken for stick insects - they are certainly wonderfully well camouflaged) and therefore young and adults of these long-lived insects may be observed together during the late summer months.

EUROPEAN CRANE FLY

(OR DADDY LONG-LEGS)

Despite their names, as adults, crane flies do not prey on mosquitoes, nor do they bite humans. But some larval crane flies are predatory and may eat mosquito larvae. Adult crane flies feed on nectar or they do not feed at all. Once they become adults, most crane fly species exist just to mate and die. Their larvae (called leatherjackets or leatherbacks because of the way they move) consume roots and other vegetation, in some cases causing damage to plants. The crane fly is considered a mild "turf pest" in some areas. Lord's Cricket Ground in London was among the places affected by them: several thousand were collected by ground staff and burned, because they caused bald patches on the wicket and the pitch took unaccustomed spin for much of the season. 16

European Owl Fly

LIBELLOIDES COCCAGUS

It's found in mountainous areas in South-Eastern Europe. She looks approximately between an ant lion, a butterfly and a dragonfly. They have long antennae with little balls on the end, and they have yellow stains on their wings. They are active during the day. After mating, the females lay their eggs under stones.

Fourteen-Spot LADYBUG

The background color ranges from cream through yellow to light orange, but not red. Usually they have 14 black, almost rectangular spots on the elytras, but only rarely there are really 14 separate spots.

Commonly, several of the spots fuse into larger markings, particularly along the midline, where they often create a shape resembling an anchor, sometimes fusing so much that the yellow disappears almost completely and render the body almost entirely black, except for 12 pale yellow spots. Their pronotum is whitish or pale yellow, with four to eight black spots. The antennae and legs are yellowish brown.

FROGHOPER

Adult froghoppers jump from plant to plant. Some species can jump up to 70 cm high. *Many species resemble leafhoppers, but can be distinguished by the possession of only a few stout spines on the back tibia, where leafhoppers have a series of small spines. Members of the family Cercopidae, they have their wings modified to form false heads at the tail end, an anti-predator adaptation. Many adult Cercopidae can bleed on purpose from their tarsi to pretend dead. (Cont.)*

FROGHOPER
(continued)

The froth serves a number of purposes. It hides the nymph from the view of predators and parasites, it insulates against heat and cold, thus providing thermal control and also moisture control. Without the froth the insect would quickly dry up. The nymphs pierce plants and sucks sap causing very little damage, much of the filtered fluids go into the production of the froth, which has an acrid taste, deterring predators. A few species are serious agricultural pests.

Grasshopper

Grasshopper

To distinguish the grasshopper from bush crickets or katydids, it is sometimes referred to as the short-horned grasshopper. Species that change color and behavior at high population densities are called locusts.

They have mandibles that tear and cut off his food. Those species that make easily heard noises usually do so by rubbing the hind femurs against the forewings or abdomen, or by snapping the wings in flight.

Grasshoppers prefer to eat grasses, leaves and cereal crops, but many grasshoppers are omnivorous.

GREEN SAWFLY

Green sawflies are distinguishable from most other Hymenoptera by the broad connection between the abdomen and the thorax, and by their caterpillar-like larvae. The common name comes from the saw-like appearance of the ovipositor, which the females use to cut into the plants where they lay their eggs. Large populations of certain sawfly species can cause substantial damage to forests and cultivated plants.

Hornet

Hornets are the largesteusocial wasps; some species can reach up to 5.6 cm in length. The true hornets make up the genus Vespa and are distinguished from other vespines by the width of the vertex (part of the head behind the eyes), which is proportionally larger in Vespa and by the anteriorly rounded gasters (the section of the abdomen behind the wasp waist). The best known species is the European hornet, about 2–3.5 cm in length, widely distributed throughout Europe, Russia, North America and Northeast Asia.

HORSE FLY

- Adult horse flies feed on nectar and sometimes pollen. Females of most species require a blood meal before they are able to reproduce. Most female horse flies feed on mammalian blood, but some species are known to feed on birds or reptiles. Some are said to attack amphibians as well.

- Larvae horse flies are predators of small invertebrates in moist environments, such as in mud on the edges of bodies of water, in damp soil, under stones, or in rotting logs.

- Mating is done in swarms, generally at hilltops. The season and time of day used for mating swarms is specific to some species. Eggs are laid on stones or vegetation, usually close to water. Just after hatching, the larvae fall into water or moist earth, feeding on invertebrates, such as snails, earthworms and other insects.

HORSE FLY (continued)

Horse fly bites are painful, the bites of large ones especially so, and more immediately and globally than that of the mosquitoes, although it still aims to escape before its victim responds. The flies are very agile and adept at flying.

Their bites may become itchy, sometimes causing a large swelling afterwards, if not treated quickly. Most species of horse flies use their knife-like mandibles to rip and slice flesh apart.

They are often not deterred by attempts at fanning them away and will persist in attacking, or even chasse their intended target, for some time.

Hornet

KLAMATH WEED BEETLE

The Klamath Weed Beetle is of the species of Hypericum and of the genus Chrysolina. Approximately 370 species of the genus Chrysolina exist worldwide in regions of North America, Europe, Turkey, Ukraine, Russia, Middle East, India, China and Brazil.

Their eggs are laid under the leaves of klamath weed (also called St John's wort) and their larvae feed at night for about a month before going underground to become adults (taking about 2 weeks), who also feed on leaves and flowers.

LEAF INSECTS

The Leaf Insects (or walking leaves) belong to the family Phylliidae that contains these extant *(still alive)* which include the most incredible leaf mimics in the world. With this perfect camouflage, they fool well their predators, like birds and spiders. They are found in South and Southeast Asia and also in Australia. There is no preferred classification of this group that contains members that are also considered to be from several different families.

MILLET SKIPPER

Pelopidas thrax is also known as the Pale Small-branded Swift, Millet Skipper or White Branded Swift. It is a butterfly belonging to the family Hesperiidae. It is found in south-eastern Europe, northern Africa and southern Asia as well as the Indonesian islands and Hawaii. In Greece, it is only known at Samos and Rhodos, where it is found on heights of 0 to 75 meters.

It has a wide head and wide separation of its antennae. The larvae are known to feed on Proso millet (*Panicum miliaceum)* in northern Africa. In some areas, it is considered an agricultural pest because its larvae can do big amounts of damage to banana and rice crops.

MOLE CRICKETS

They are quite common but we rarely see them because they are nocturnal creatures that spend most time of their lives inside long tunnels. They have powerful front legs for digging and are also good swimmers. They have an omnivorous diet, including worms, roots and leaves. They can reach up to 2 inches in length.

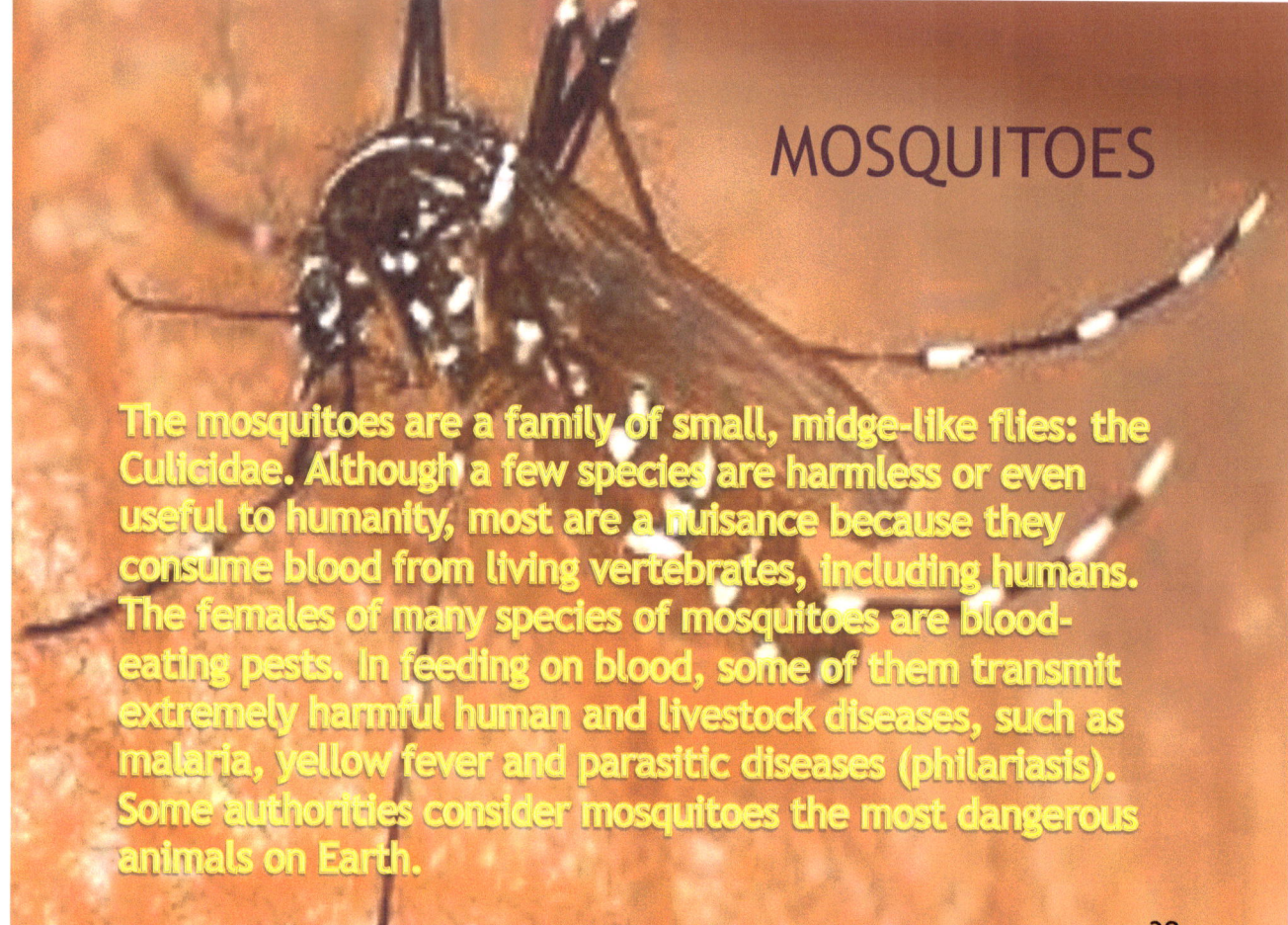

MOSQUITOES

The mosquitoes are a family of small, midge-like flies: the Culicidae. Although a few species are harmless or even useful to humanity, most are a nuisance because they consume blood from living vertebrates, including humans. The females of many species of mosquitoes are blood-eating pests. In feeding on blood, some of them transmit extremely harmful human and livestock diseases, such as malaria, yellow fever and parasitic diseases (philariasis). Some authorities consider mosquitoes the most dangerous animals on Earth.

TWO-SPOT BLACK LADYBUG

Chilocorus stigma, commonly known as the twice-stabbed lady beetle, is a native resident of the United States and Canada but does not live west of the Sierra Nevada. The two-stabbed lady beetle Chilocorus orbus is found widespread in California. It also lives in Oceania and has been introduced to Hawaii. It is shiny black in color, and there is one red spot on each elytra. The remainder of the body is black as well, but the abdomen is either yellow or red in color.

33

ORIENTAL PAPER WASP

Paper wasps are 0.7 to 1 inch long wasps that gather fibers from dead wood and plant stems. They mix it with saliva to construct water-resistant nests that look like gray or brown papery. Paper wasps are also sometimes called **"umbrella wasps"**, due to the distinctive design of their nests that stay suspended from solid structures.

Rhinoceros Beetle

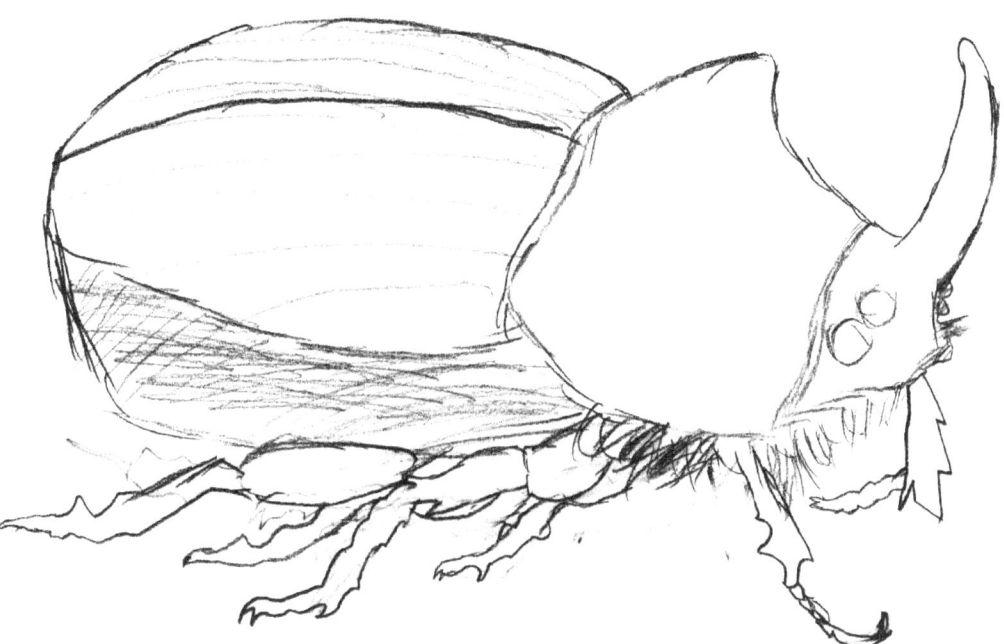

Pedro Lima

RHINOCEROS BEETLE
(*Oryctophileurus guerrai*)

Like the other species of the genus, this new species might be rare or has a cryptic way of life. The Rhinoceros Beetle, named *Oryctophileurus guerrai*, measures about 2 cm long by 1 cm wide.

This new specie is found in Bolivia and was named after Fernando Fideo Guerra, for his lifetime commitment to the investigation of the Bolivian fauna. His participation in the actual survey in the southern Bolivian Andes has led to the discovery and description of several previously unknown taxa, and he was also the first to collect an individual of *Oryctophileurus guerrai*.

Oryctophileurus guerrai resembles known species *O. armicollis*, but can be distinguished by the distance between the inner teeth on the dorsal pronotal protuberance, and in females by the inner teeth separated by only a small difference.

ROBER FLY

From the family **Asilidae**, the robber flies are also called "assassin flies": the victim is bitten and injected with saliva that contains a nerve poison that causes paralysis. They are powerfully built, bristly flies with short, sharp, stout sucking mouthparts. They are named "robber fly" because of their notoriously aggressive predatory habits; they feed mainly on other insects and they largely wait in ambush and catch their prey in flight. They don't fly really fast but they are capable of carrying sizeable prey. More than 7 thousand species have been found around the world.

ROSE APHIDS

Rose aphids are distributed worldwide, they can become serious pests, because they don't only suck the juices of their hosts plants but they also spread viral infections. They overwinter as eggs; these then hatch during Spring, and if left unchecked, can quickly reproduce to form expensive colonies. Rose aphids produce honeydew, a sugary substance much favored by ants. If enough of it builds up on the leaves, a black mold often develops on them. Wile ants will foster the aphids, other insects, such as ladybugs, hoverflies, lacewings, and parasitic wasps are their main predators. They are found worldwide and are well known by gardeners everywhere.

SCALE INSECT

There are about 8,000 described species of scale insects. Scale insects change a lot in their appearance and from very small creatures that grow beneath wax covers, to shiny pearl-like objects, to creatures covered with mealy wax. Adult female scales are almost always immobile and permanently attached to the plant they have parasitized. They secrete a waxy coating for defense; this coating causes them to resemble reptilian scales or fish scales, from where their common name.

SILVERFISH

Lepisma saccharina, commonly known as a "silverfish", is a small wingless insect of the order Thysanura. Its common name derives from the animal's silvery light grey and blue color, combined with the fish-like appearance of its movements. The scientific name indicates the silverfish's diet of carbohydrates such as sugar or starches. It changed little since it first appeared around 300 million years ago. They can be little pests to some households because they eat many items like paper, cotton, linen, wallpaper, glue, etc.

SMALL ELEPHANT HAWKMOTH

- As its name suggests, the "small" elephant hawkmoth is not as large if compared to the elephant hawkmoth.

- This species is found in Britain and Ireland but also extends its range all across Europe, Russia, China, northern parts of the Indian subcontinent, as well as Japan and Korea.

- Their larvae eat a lot of species of bedstraw and willow herb. When adult, the moth pupates to emerge during the Summer.

SMALL TORTOISESHELL

- It occupies a wide range of natural habitats (gardens, urban parks, groves), except for dense forest, up to more than 3000 m above sea level. The caterpillars feed on stinging nettle and small nettles, as do those of several Nymphalid butterflies. Adults feed on nectar. The species has one of the longest seasons of any Eurasian butterfly, extending from early Spring to late Autumn.

- Adults overwinter in hibernation, emerging on the first warm sunny days of the year to mate and breed. In southern parts of the range there may be two broods each year, but northern insects are inhibited by long Summer day length from breeding a second time. The males establish territories and can be seen flying up into the sky to challenge intruders and rivals.

42

This is a species often found in gardens. The adult is wonderful, with its dark body and red and yellow wings, which have a row of blue dots around the rear edge. However under the wings it's not so colorful. When threatened, resting individuals rapidly open their wings, presenting the dramatic display of colors. This can frighten away young or inexperienced birds.

SOUTHERN HAWKER

(DRAGONFLY)

The **Southern Hawker** (Aeshna Cyanea) is a 70 millimeters long species of hawker dragonfly. It is large, with a long body. It has green and black spots on its body, and the male also has blue spots on the abdomen. The Southern Hawker breeds near ponds, lakes and streams, but will wander widely to catch prey, and is also seen in gardens and open woodland. This is a curious species and will approach people. It is found all across Europe and its aquatic larvae takes about 3 years to develop.

Southern Wood Ant
(Formica rufa)

The nests of these ants are large, dome-shaped mounds constructed out of dry plants (grass, twigs, or conifer needles) or soil and often built against a rotting stump. They usually do them in woodland clearings where the sun's rays can reach them. Large colonies may have 100,000 to 400,000 workers and 100 queens (egg-producing females): *F. rufa* is polygynous ("plural marriage"). They often re-adopt post-nuptial queens from their own mother colony, leading to old, multi gallery nests. These colonies can be very big, often measuring several meters in height and diameter.

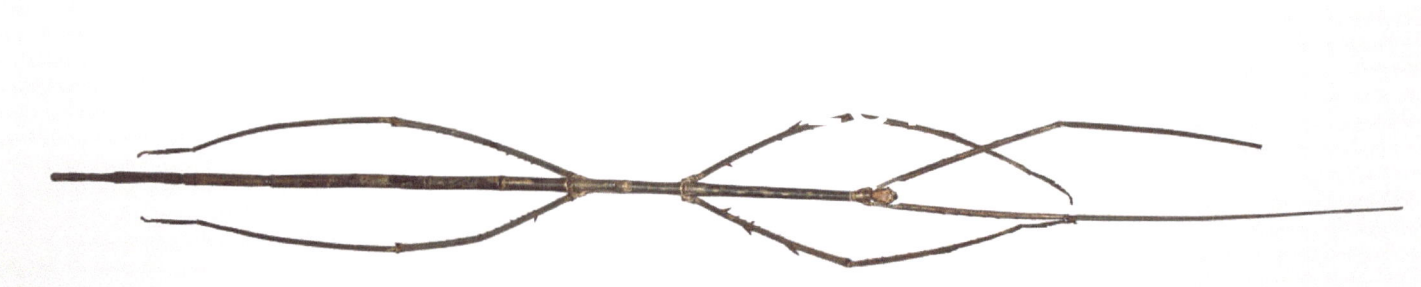

The Phasmatodea is an order of plant-eating insects known as "stick insects" (in Europe, Australia and Asia), walking sticks or "stick-bugs" (in the United States and Canada). Their common name is derived from the Ancient Greek (φάσμα - "phasma"), meaning an apparition or phantom, and refers to the resemblance of many species to sticks or leaves. Phasmids ("ghost insects" or "leaf insects") are generally from the family Phylliidae. Their natural camouflage can make them extremely difficult to spot. They can be found all over the world in warmer zones, especially the tropics and subtropics. The greatest diversity is found in Southeast Asia and South America, followed by Australia. But they also have a considerable presence in the continental United States, especially in the Southeast.

STONEFLY

© AndrewWilliams/CritterZone.com

- Plecoptera is an order of insects commonly known as "stoneflies". There are some 3,500 described species around the world found in both the Southern and Northern hemispheres, except for Antarctica, with new species still being discovered. Stoneflies are believed to be one of the most primitive groups of the Neoptera family (winged insects that can flex their wings over their abdomens): the modern diversity apparently is of Mesozoic origin.

- They have aquatic larvae which hide under stones on the bed of lakes, streams and small rivers. When matured, the larvae crawl out of the water where the adults will emerge. They have 2 pairs of wings that are kept folded back over their body when they are resting. All species are intolerant of water pollution, so their presence in a stream or still water is usually an indicator of good water quality.

Giant or Stream Lacewing

The Giant Lacewing is a large member of the order Neuroptera (contains 4,000 species) that lays its eggs in vegetation on the edges of running water. When the larvae hatch, they are predators on a wide variety of small invertebrates. Its wingspan can go up to 2 inches (50 mm). It can be found in late Spring and early Summer in damp areas near rivers and streams. It is distributed across central Europe, but being mostly crepuscular in its behavior, it is not often seen during the day.

48

Two-Banded Longhorn Beetle

Longhorn beetles are very distinctive beetles, with long swept back antennae. Their eggs are laid in dead wood, plus other places containing trees and shrubs. Many species are easy to identify. They are frequently found on flowers such as hogweed, hawthorn and wild roses, or walking about on dead wood or trees. At present, there are records for 29 species of longhorn beetles. The two-banded longhorn beetle, is one of the most common in Europe, Turkey and the Caucasus, but it is absent from the far north-east of Europe and some offshore islands, such as Malta. It may reach 22 mm long and can be distinguished by the two prominent yellow bands on each of their elytras (pair of old wings recovering the new ones), but up to 17 different patterns have already been recognized.

WASP BEETLE

The Wasp Beetle, is a wasp-mimicking longhorn beetle species in the genus Clytus. It reaches 9–18 millimeters in length, and flies well in sunshine from May to July, often visiting flowers for pollen and nectar. It is harmless but is protected by its wasp-like colours and movements. The larvae live in dead wood. It also emanates a wasp buzz-like noise when threatened. They can be seen wandering around on flowers, from late Spring to early Summer, and they are easily mistaken for a wasp.

Water Scorpion

- Water Scorpion **is one** of the approximately 150 species of aquatic invertebrates of the family Nepidae (order of Hemiptera). The water scorpion resembles a land scorpion in certain ways: it has scythe-like front legs adapted for seizing prey and a long, thin, whip-like structure at its posterior end. This "tail", made up of two attached respiratory tubes, is extended above the surface of the water, enabling the animal to take in air.

- Found worldwide, water scorpions live primarily along the bottom edges of ditches and muddy ponds, where they hide among dead, water-logged leaves and other plant debris to ambush their prey. They rarely move much in open water because they are poor swimmers. Adults lay their eggs in the fractures of debris and on the branches of water plants.

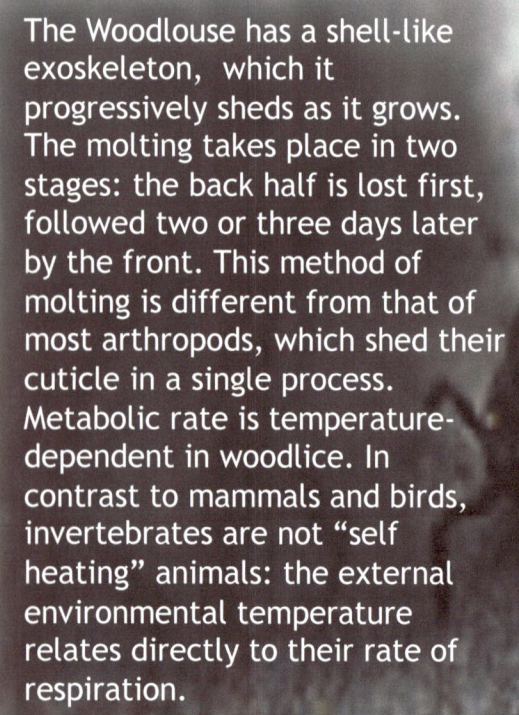

WOODLOUSE

The Woodlouse has a shell-like exoskeleton, which it progressively sheds as it grows. The molting takes place in two stages: the back half is lost first, followed two or three days later by the front. This method of molting is different from that of most arthropods, which shed their cuticle in a single process. Metabolic rate is temperature-dependent in woodlice. In contrast to mammals and birds, invertebrates are not "self heating" animals: the external environmental temperature relates directly to their rate of respiration.

A female woodlouse will keep fertilized eggs in a "marsupium" under her body until they hatch into small, white offsprings. The mother then appears to "give birth" to her babies. Females are also capable of reproducing asexually. Despite being crustaceans, like lobsters or crabs, woodlice are said to have an unpleasant taste, similar to "strong urine".

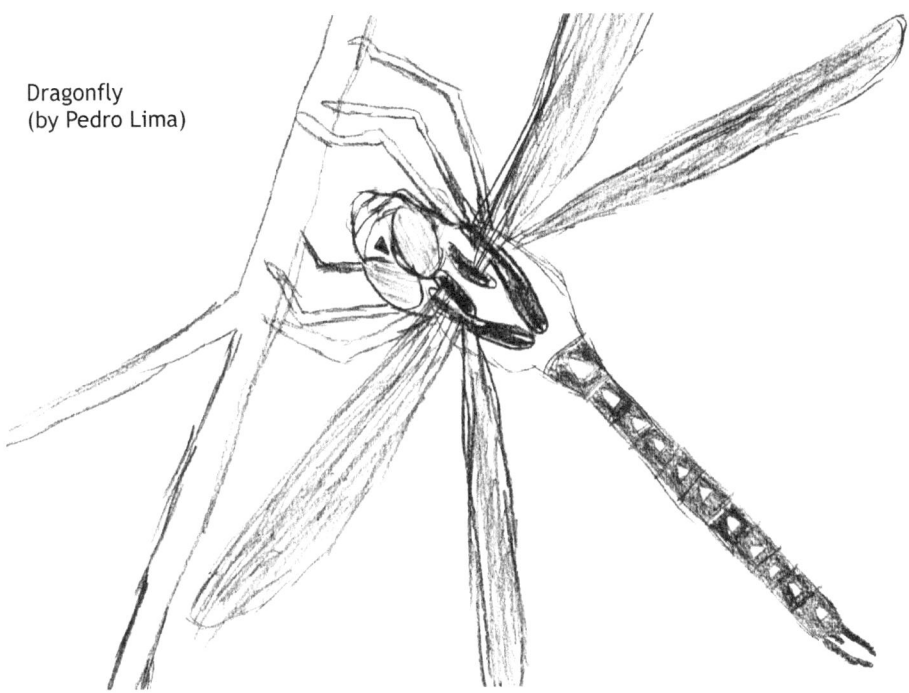

Dragonfly
(by Pedro Lima)

Ancient Dragonflies

23,5 cm

95,3 cm

The dragonflies were this BIG: 60 million years ago...